THE OFFICIAL
ENGLAND
ANNUAL 2024

g

A Grange Publication

Written by Andy Greeves | Designed by Stacey Potter & Adam Wilsher

© 2023. Published by Grange Communications Ltd., Edinburgh, under licence from The Football Association.

Printed in the EU.

ISBN 978-1-915879-18-9

CONTENTS

6   2023 FIFA Women's World Cup Review

12   England Senior Men's Profile

14   Gareth Southgate Timeline

16   England Men's Senior Team Profiles

22   England Senior Women's Profile

24   Sarina Wiegman Timeline

26   England Women's Senior Team Profiles

32   Crossword

33   Wordsearch

34   Harry Kane: Record Breaker!

38   Women's Finalissima

40   England Quiz

42   2023 UEFA U-21 Championship

46   2023 Men's U-20 World Cup

48   2023 UEFA U-17 Championships

50   2023 Round-Up

52   Guess the Goalscorer

56   Behind the Scenes at the Home of England

58   UEFA Euro 2024

60   Quiz/Puzzle Answers

62   Spot the Players

WELCOME TO THE OFFICIAL ENGLAND ANNUAL 2024

What a journey it has been for England's various teams in recent years. Following up on their success at UEFA Women's Euro 2022, Sarina Wiegman's Lionesses reached their first-ever FIFA Women's World Cup Final in 2023. Gareth Southgate's Three Lions were in a strong position to reach UEFA Euro 2024 at the time of writing – a competition they reached the final of back in 2021 (the delayed UEFA Euro 2020) – with skipper Harry Kane banging in the goals! And there has been success at development level with Lee Carsley's Young Lions having won the 2023 UEFA European Under-21 Championship.

In this Annual, we review the 2023 FIFA Women's World Cup and the 2023 UEFA European Under-21 Championship as well as the Women's Finalissima, 2023 FIFA Under-20 World Cup and the UEFA Women's Under-17 Euros.

We profile the players who currently make up the England Men's and Women's senior squads and explore the key strikes that saw Kane become the Three Lions' all-time record goalscorer.

We also look ahead to UEFA Euro 2024, hoping Gareth Southgate's team can go one better than three years earlier and win the competition!

Elsewhere, there are other features, quizzes, games and plenty more to entertain England fans of all ages!

Enjoy this Annual and COME ON ENGLAND!

#ThreeLions #Lionesses

2023 FIFA WOMEN'S WORLD CUP REVIEW

We look back on the Lionesses' incredible run to the 2023 FIFA Women's World Cup Final.

GROUP PHASE

ENGLAND 1 HAITI 0

ENGLAND LINE-UP: Earps, Bronze, Bright, Carter, Greenwood, Stanway, Walsh, Toone, Kelly, Russo (Daly 76), Hemp (James 61)

A 29th-minute Georgia Stanway penalty got England off to a winning start in their 2023 FIFA Women's World Cup Group D opener. The Bayern Munich midfielder had to re-take the spot kick after VAR ruled Haiti 'keeper Kerly Theus had stepped off her line too early when saving the first attempt.

The Lionesses' defence were kept busy for the remainder of the match as Lyon's teenage star midfielder Melchie Dumornay and her Haiti teammates - appearing at the tournament for the first time - pushed for an equaliser, but they were unable to find a way through.

ENGLAND 1 DENMARK 0

ENGLAND LINE-UP: Earps, Bronze, Bright, Greenwood, Daly, Stanway, Walsh (Coombs 38), Toone (Hemp 76), Kelly, Russo (England 76), James

The Lionesses made it back-to-back wins as Lauren James' sixth-minute strike proved the difference between them and the Danes in Sydney. The Chelsea forward - who was 21 at the time - became England's second youngest Women's World Cup goalscorer, after Jill Scott, when she curled the ball past Lene Christensen in the Denmark goal.

Sarina Wiegman's side suffered a blow when midfielder Keira Walsh was stretchered off with a knee injury before half-time but despite late pressure from Denmark, who hit the post, they held on for all three points.

CHINA 1 ENGLAND 6

ENGLAND LINE-UP: Earps, Carter, Bright, Greenwood, Bronze, Stanway, Zelem, Daly, James (Toone 81), Russo (England 71), Hemp (Kelly 71)

England capped off their group games in style with a 6-1 thrashing of China to progress to the knockout phase of the Women's World Cup.

Alessia Russo opened the scoring after just four minutes and Lauren Hemp doubled their lead shortly before the half-hour mark. James netted her second of the tournament close to the break but China pulled it back to 3-1 in the second half when Wang Shuang scored from the penalty spot after a Lucy Bronze handball.

Another stunning strike from James on 65 minutes put the game out of China's reach. And Wiegman's side weren't finished yet... Chloe Kelly and Rachel Daly also got on the scoresheet to round off a dominant display from the Lionesses in Adelaide.

FINAL GROUP D TABLE

		P	W	D	L	GF	GA	GD	PTS
1	England (Q)	3	3	0	0	8	1	+7	9
2	Denmark(Q)	3	2	0	1	3	1	+2	6
3	China PR	3	1	0	2	2	7	-5	3
4	Haiti	3	0	0	3	0	4	-4	0

KNOCKOUT PHASE

ENGLAND 0 NIGERIA 0
(AFTER EXTRA-TIME – ENGLAND WIN 4-2 ON PENALTIES)

ENGLAND LINE-UP: Earps, Carter, Bright, Greenwood, Bronze, Stanway, Walsh (Zelem 120), Daly, James, Russo (Kelly 88), Hemp (England 105)

England beat Nigeria in a penalty shootout to reach the Women's World Cup quarter-finals after a hard-fought encounter finished goalless after extra-time in Brisbane.

Nigeria had the better chances in open play, hitting the crossbar twice, while Chelsea striker James saw red on 87 minutes for a stamp on Michelle Alozie. But Wiegman's ten players held firm in defence during extra-time to take the game to penalties.

Stanway fired wide with the opening spot-kick but Bethany England, Rachel Daly, Alex Greenwood and Chloe Kelly made no mistake as the Lionesses came out on top in the shootout.

ENGLAND 2 COLOMBIA 1

ENGLAND LINE-UP: Earps, Carter, Bright, Greenwood, Bronze, Stanway, Walsh, Daly, Toone, Russo (Kelly 85), Hemp (England 90)

Strikes from Hemp and Russo saw England book themselves a place in the final four of the competition in front of 75,000 fans in Sydney.

The Lionesses went behind after Colombia's Leicy Santos looped the ball over Earps on 44 minutes. But Hemp's close-range finish after Catalina Perez spilled Russo's initial effort on the stroke of half-time saw them go in level at the break.

England had momentum as the second half got underway and a defensive error from Colombia allowed Arsenal striker Russo to drill the ball into the bottom corner for England's second just after the hour mark to seal the win for Wiegman's side.

AUSTRALIA 1 ENGLAND 3

ENGLAND LINE-UP: Earps, Carter, Bright, Greenwood, Bronze, Stanway, Walsh, Daly, Toone (Charles 90), Russo (Kelly 87), Hemp

A confident display saw England beat co-hosts Australia 3-1 to reach their first-ever FIFA Women's World Cup Final. Toone opened the Lionesses' account with a sweet shot into the top corner in the 36th-minute but the Matildas' Sam Kerr equalised with a stunning, 25-yard strike just after the hour mark.

Hemp restored England's lead with just under 20 minutes to play - her third goal of the tournament - and Russo sealed victory for the Lionesses when she netted her third competition strike too with less than five minutes of normal time remaining.

SPAIN 1 ENGLAND 0

**FIFA WOMEN'S WORLD CUP 2023 - FINAL
20 AUGUST 2023
STADIUM AUSTRALIA. SYDNEY**

ENGLAND LINE-UP: Earps, Carter, Bright, Greenwood, Bronze, Stanway, Walsh, Daly (Kelly 45), Toone (England 87), Russo (James 45), Hemp

There was heartbreak for the Lionesses in Sydney as they lost 1-0 to Spain in the FIFA Women's World Cup Final.

It could have been a different story had Hemp's powerful shot on 15 minutes, which hit the crossbar, been struck an inch or two lower. Spain goalkeeper Cata Coll also denied the Lionesses on a number of occasions over the 90 minutes.

Spain's captain Olga Carmona broke the deadlock with a precise strike into the bottom corner on 29 minutes and the Spanish could have doubled their advantage just before the break but Irene Paredes' shot went wide.

Wiegman's side had a better spell in possession in the second half. When Earps saved a 70th-minute penalty from Jenni Hermoso, after Walsh was adjudged to have handled in the box, it gave the Lionesses belief that perhaps this would be their night. They pushed hard for an equaliser, but sadly it wasn't to be and they finished the tournament as runners-up.

ENGLAND SENIOR

HEAD COACH

CAPTAIN

GARETH SOUTHGATE

HARRY KANE

RECORDS

TOP SCORER:

58*
HARRY KANE

MOST CAPS:

125

FIRST INTERNATIONAL:

PETER SHILTON

INTERNATIONAL
FOOT-BALL MATCH,
(Association Rules.)
ENGLAND v. SCOTLAND,
WEST OF SCOTLAND CRICKET GROUND,
Hamilton Crescent, Partick,
SATURDAY, 30th November, 1872, at 2 p.m.

ADMISSION—ONE SHILLING.

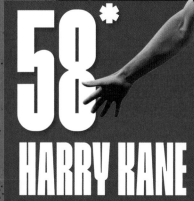

0-0 V SCOTLAND (A)
30 NOVEMBER 1872

MEN'S PROFILE

13-0 V IRELAND (A)
18 FEBRUARY 1882

TOURNAMENT PERFORMANCES

UEFA EUROPEAN CHAMPIONSHIP APPEARANCES:

10

FIFA WORLD CUP APPEARANCES:

17

BEST PERFORMANCE:

RUNNERS-UP, 2020

BEST PERFORMANCE:

WINNERS 1966

UEFA NATIONS LEAGUE FINAL TOURNAMENT APPEARANCES:

1

BEST PERFORMANCE:

THIRD-PLACE, 2019

*Figure correct as of August 2023

TIMELINE

1970
Gareth was born in Watford on 3 September 1970.

1988
Gareth joined Crystal Palace's youth set up where he worked his way into the first team.

1993
After being named Eagles captain, Gareth and his teammates achieved promotion to the Premier League at the end of 1993/94.

1995
Following 191 appearances for Palace during which he scored 22 goals, Gareth departed Selhurst Park to sign for Aston Villa in the summer of 1995. On 12 December that year, he made his England debut as a substitute in a 1-1 friendly draw with Portugal at Wembley Stadium.

1996
Gareth was selected in Terry Venables' 22-man squad for UEFA Euro 1996 and started in all five of England's matches at the tournament.

GARETH SOUTHGATE

1998

At the 1998 FIFA World Cup Gareth played in two matches, including the round of 16 tie with Argentina. Later that year he scored his first England goal in a 3-0 away win in Luxembourg.

2000

Gareth came on as a late substitute for Paul Scholes in England's Group A clash with Romania at UEFA Euro 2000, which marked an appearance at his third major tournament for the Three Lions.

2001

In the summer of 2001 Gareth left Aston Villa for Middlesbrough. He continued to play for England, making three international appearances that year.

2002

Gareth was named in Sven-Göran Eriksson's squad for the 2002 FIFA World Cup but didn't feature in the tournament. He won his 50th England cap in a 1-1 draw with Portugal at Villa Park in September that year.

2003

Southgate scored his second and final goal for England in 2-1 friendly victory over South Africa in May. He made his last competitive appearance for the Three Lions in a 2-1 win against Slovakia a month later in a UEFA Euro 2004 qualifier.

2004

With Southgate as their captain, Middlesbrough beat Bolton Wanderers in the Football League Cup final in February 2004. The following month Southgate made his final appearance in an England shirt, in a 1-0 friendly defeat in Sweden.

2006

After 638 appearances and 35 goals, Gareth retired from playing club football in the summer of 2006, when he became Middlesbrough manager, a role he held until 2009.

2013

Gareth's next football challenge saw him appointed as the Head Coach of England Men's U21s in August 2013. He led the team to qualify for the UEFA European U21 Championship finals in 2015.

2016

Following Sam Allardyce's resignation, Gareth was put in temporary charge of the Men's Senior team for fixtures against Malta, Slovenia, Scotland and Spain. He was appointed manager in November 2016 on a four-year contract.

2018

England reached the semi-finals of the World Cup in Russia, where they were knocked out by Croatia. En route to the last four, the Three Lions triumphed in a penalty shootout at the tournament for the first time, as they beat Colombia in the round of 16.

2019

In recognition of England's efforts and achievements, Gareth was named as an Officer of the Most Excellent Order of the British Empire (OBE) in the New Year's Honours list.

2021

At the delayed UEFA Euro 2020, England topped Group D and beat Germany, Ukraine and Denmark to reach their first major competition final in 55 years. Italy triumphed 3-2 on penalties after the Wembley Stadium final finished 1-1 after extra-time.

2022

Gareth's Three Lions won their group at the winter World Cup in Qatar with wins over Iran and Wales and a draw with the United States. They beat Senegal 3-0 in the round of 16 but lost to France in the quarter-finals. After the tournament, Gareth confirmed he would remain as manager until after UEFA Euro 2024.

GOALKEEPERS

NICK POPE

Position: Goalkeeper
Date/Place of Birth: 19 April 1992 - Soham
England Debut: 6 June 2018 v Costa Rica (H)

From his debut in 2018 through until the end of 2022, Nick had won 10 senior caps for England and made the 23-man squad for the Three Lions' appearances at the 2018 and 2022 FIFA World Cups.

The former Charlton Athletic and Burnley goalkeeper, who moved to Newcastle United in 2022, made his competitive debut for England against Kosovo in a UEFA Euro 2020 qualifier in November 2019. He set an individual England goalkeeping record by going his first 498 minutes at senior international level without conceding a goal before shipping an effort from Jakub Moder in a 2-1 win over Poland in March 2021.

JORDAN PICKFORD

Position: Goalkeeper
Date/Place of Birth:
7 March 1994 - Washington
England Debut:
10 November 2017 v Germany (H)

A regular in the England team since making his international debut in 2017, Jordan earnt his 50th cap in the Three Lions' 2022 FIFA World Cup quarter-final defeat to France in December 2022. He played every minute of their campaign in Qatar, putting in some fine performances and keeping three clean sheets. Jordan also impressed at UEFA Euro 2020 - becoming the first goalkeeper in history to keep shut outs in the first five games of the competition - and at the 2018 World Cup, where he made the decisive save to deny Carlos Bacca's spot kick for Colombia in the round of 16 to help England win their first-ever World Cup penalty shootout.

AARON RAMSDALE

Position: Goalkeeper
Date/Place of Birth:
14 May 1998 - Stoke-on-Trent
England Debut: 15 November 2021
v San Marino (A)

After playing for England at U18, U20 and U21 level, Aaron made his senior debut in a World Cup qualifier against San Marino in November 2021. He'd received a late call-up for that summer's delayed UEFA Euro 2020 after Dean Henderson withdrew through injury one game into the tournament, but didn't feature. In June 2022, Gareth Southgate selected the Arsenal stopper for two UEFA Nations League games where he kept a clean sheet in a goalless draw against Italy. The England manager also named the goalkeeper in his 26-man squad for the 2022 FIFA World Cup in Qatar.

SAM JOHNSTONE

Position: Goalkeeper
Date/Place of Birth: Preston
- 25 March 1993
England Debut: 6 June 2021
v Romania (H)

Sam won his first England senior call-up in March 2021 and went on to make his debut three months later, keeping a clean sheet in a 1-0 friendly victory against Romania. Gareth Southgate called upon him again for two FIFA World Cup qualifiers against Andorra in autumn 2021 and Sam didn't disappoint, keeping two more shut outs. The shot stopper was a member of England's victorious squad at the 2010 UEFA European U-17 Championship and he also helped the Young Lions reach the semi-finals of the European U-19 Championship two years later.

DEFENDERS

KYLE WALKER

Position: Defender
Date/Place of Birth:
28 May 1990 - Sheffield
England Debut:
12 November 2011 v Spain (H)

Kyle has played an integral role in the Three Lions' defence in recent years with 76 senior caps to his name at the time of writing. He was named Man of the Match on his England debut, a 1-0 win against Sweden in 2011, and a decade later the right-back's performances during UEFA Euro 2020 earnt him a place in the Team of the Tournament as the Three Lions reached the final of the competition. Kyle was selected for Gareth Southgate's squad for the 2022 FIFA World Cup and featured in three games including their quarter-final defeat to France.

JOHN STONES

Position: Defender
Date/Place of Birth:
28 May 1994 - Barnsley
England Debut:
30 May 2014 v Peru (H)

Previously capped at U19, U20 and U21 level, John has been a regular in the England team at their last three major tournaments. At the 2018 FIFA World Cup he featured in every game and scored twice in a 6-1 win over Panama in the group stage and the centre-back also played all seven matches as the Three Lions reached the final of Euro 2020. Named in Gareth Southgate's squad for the 2022 FIFA World Cup in Qatar too, John played an important role in England's defence during the tournament. A start against North Macedonia in June 2023 took Stones' cap tally to 67.

HARRY MAGUIRE

Position: Defender
Date/Place of Birth:
5 March 1993 - Sheffield
England Debut:
8 October 2017 v Lithuania (A)

Harry's impressive performances at the 2022 FIFA World Cup saw the England centre-back named in the Team of the Tournament. He received the same recognition at UEFA Euro 2020 where the defender played in England's final group game and all of their knockout matches, including the final. He smashed home his penalty in the resulting shootout against Italy, but England went on to lose 3-2. After playing against Malta and North Macedonia in UEFA Euro 2024 qualifying matches in June 2023, Harry had 57 senior caps to his name and was the Three Lions' highest scoring defender with seven goals.

KIERAN TRIPPIER

Position: Defender
Date/Place of Birth: 19 September 1990 - Bury
England Debut: 13 June 2017 v France (A)

Kieran featured in all three of England's group games at the 2022 FIFA World Cup in his third major international tournament. The Newcastle United right-back is eight shy of 50 Three Lions' appearances at the time of writing, and his perfectly executed free-kick to give England the lead in their semi-final clash with Croatia at the 2018 World Cup is hard to forget. Kieran also played five matches at UEFA Euro 2020 and supplied the assist for Luke Shaw's goal in the final against Italy.

REECE JAMES

Position: Defender
Date/Place of Birth: 8 December 1999 - Redbridge
England Debut: 8 October 2020 v Wales (H)

The brother of Lionesses star Lauren James, Reece offers great versatility to England head coach Gareth Southgate. The Chelsea player has appeared at both right-back, left-back, central midfield and as a right-sided wing-back during his international career so far. With six senior England appearances to his name prior to UEFA Euro 2020, the Chelsea player started his first senior tournament match for the Three Lions against Scotland in the group stage of the competition. He had won 16 caps for England in total by the end of August 2023.

TYRONE MINGS

Position: **Defender**
Date/Place of Birth: **13 March 1993 - Bath**
England Debut: **14 October 2019 v Bulgaria (A)**

Tyrone came on as a substitute in England's 4-0 win in Malta on 16 June 2023 to win his 18th senior international cap. He started in the Three Lions' first two UEFA Euro 2020 Group D fixtures, helping to keep clean sheets against Croatia and Scotland, while he came on as a substitute against the Czech Republic at the tournament. Tyrone has scored two international goals to date including a late header in England's 3-0 friendly win over Ivory Coast in March 2022.

LUKE SHAW

Position: **Defender**
Date/Place of Birth: **12 July 1995 - Kingston upon Thames**
England Debut: **5 March 2014 v Denmark (H)**

Luke started all five of the Three Lions' matches at the 2022 FIFA World Cup and assisted Jude Bellingham's goal in the 6-2 defeat of Iran in their opening game. An experienced left-back, the Manchester United player first featured in the England senior team in February 2014 and started for the side against Costa Rica in their Group D fixture in that summer's World Cup. At UEFA Euro 2020 Luke made three assists in six appearances and scored against Italy in the final – his first of three international goals at the time of writing.

TRENT ALEXANDER-ARNOLD

Position: **Defender**
Date/Place of Birth: **7 October 1998 - Liverpool**
England Debut: **7 June 2018 v Costa Rica (H)**

Trent made his England debut in a warm-up match against Costa Rica, before starting in the 1-0 Group G defeat to Belgium at the 2018 FIFA World Cup. Trent missed out on UEFA Euro 2020 through injury but returned to the England fold for 2022 FIFA World Cup qualifying matches in September 2021. He travelled to the tournament finals with the Three Lions' squad and came on as a substitute for Kyle Walker in their 3-0 group stage victory over Wales. The 2019 Ballon d'Or nominee scored his second international goal in a 4-0 victory over Malta in a Euro 2024 qualifier in June 2023.

BEN CHILWELL

Position: **Defender**
Date/Place of Birth: **21 December 1996 - Milton Keynes**
England Debut: **11 September 2018 v Switzerland (H)**

Ben has been an important member of Gareth Southgate's England squads since his first inclusion back in September 2018. By the end of August 2023, he had featured in 18 matches, scoring his first international goal in October 2021 in a 5-0 victory over Andorra in a 2022 FIFA World Cup qualifier. An unused substitute during the delayed UEFA Euro 2020, when England made the final, Southgate praised the attitude of Ben and the Three Lions' other non-playing squad members for helping create such a good spirit in the camp.

MARC GUEHI

Position: **Defender**
Date/Place of Birth: **13 July 2000 - Abidjan, Ivory Coast**
England Debut: **26 March 2022 v Switzerland (H)**

Marc received his first senior England call-up in March 2022, making his debut in a 2-1 friendly win over Switzerland at Wembley Stadium. Prior to that he'd captained the Young Lions to the final of the UEFA European Under-17 Championship in May 2017 and scored in the FIFA U-17 World Cup final victory over Spain in October of that year. Marc went on to be capped at U19, U20 and U21 level for England before making the step up to the senior team for whom the defender had made four appearances at the time of writing.

MIDFIELDERS

JUDE BELLINGHAM

Position: Midfielder
Date/Place of Birth: 29 June 2003
- Stourbridge
England Debut: 12 November 2020
v Republic of Ireland (H)

Jude's first senior England goal came against Iran in the Three Lions' opening group fixture at the 2022 FIFA World Cup. The midfielder's header opened England's account and he went on to play an important role in Gareth Southgate's side at the tournament, starting in all five matches. The attack-minded player, who completed a big money move to Spanish giants Real Madrid in June 2023, had made 24 senior international appearances at the time of writing and was previously capped at U15, U16, U17 and U21 level.

JORDAN HENDERSON

Position: Midfielder
Date/Place of Birth: 17 June 1990
- Sunderland
England Debut: 17 November 2010
v France (H)

A two-time England Player of the Year, Jordan's inclusion in Gareth Southgate's squad for the 2022 FIFA World Cup saw him compete in his sixth major senior international tournament. The Liverpool midfielder scored his first ever World Cup goal in Qatar, in the Three Lions' 3-0 victory over Senegal in the round of 16 to bring his senior England strike tally to three in 77 appearances at the time of writing. In June 2023, Jordan was in the starting XI for back-to-back UEFA Euro 2024 qualifying victories over Malta and North Macedonia.

DECLAN RICE

Position: Midfielder
Date/Place of Birth: 14 January 1999
- Kingston upon Thames
England Debut: 22 March 2019
v Czech Republic (H)

Declan played a key role in the heart of midfield for England at the 2022 FIFA World Cup, starting all five of their matches. The Londoner, who led West Ham United to UEFA Europa Conference League victory in June 2023, switched his international allegiance from the Republic of Ireland to England in February 2019 and was impressive as the Three Lions marched to the final of UEFA Euro 2020. At the time of writing, Declan had earnt 43 senior caps and scored three goals for the Three Lions — against Iceland in November 2020, in a 4-0 win in Hungary in September 2021 and in a Euro 2024 qualifying victory over Italy in March 2023.

MASON MOUNT

Position: Midfielder
Date/Place of Birth: 10 January 1999 - Portsmouth
England Debut: 6 September 2019 v Bulgaria (H)

Mason has earnt 36 senior England caps and scored five international goals at the time of writing. A product of Chelsea's youth academy, he represented his country at various levels between U16 and U21 before Gareth Southgate called him up to the senior squad in 2018. The midfielder made his debut as a substitute in a UEFA Euro 2020 qualifier against Bulgaria in September 2019 and less than two years later he was a key figure in the Three Lions' squad at UEFA Euro 2020. Twice Chelsea's Player of the Year, Mason was also included in the England squad for the 2022 FIFA World Cup and appeared in four games.

JAMES MADDISON

Position: Midfielder
Date/Place of Birth: 23 November 1996 – Coventry
England Debut: 14 November 2019 (H) v Montenegro

James made his senior debut for England as a substitute for Alex Oxlade-Chamberlain in a 7-0 win over Montenegro at Wembley Stadium in November 2019. He added to his caps tally in 2023 as he started in the 2-0 victory over Ukraine at Wembley Stadium and the 4-0 win in Malta. The former Norwich City player has won nine England U21s caps to his name and was included in the 23-man squad for the 2019 UEFA European Under-21 Championships.

KALVIN PHILLIPS

Position: Midfielder
Date/Place of Birth: 2 December 1995 - Leeds
England Debut: 8 September 2020 v Denmark (A)

Just nine months after making his England debut, Kalvin had secured himself a regular spot in the Three Lions' midfield as he started all seven UEFA Euro 2020 matches. His impressive campaign led to him being named England's 2020-21 Men's Player of the Year and in July 2022, reigning Premier League champions Manchester City paid Leeds United a reported £42m for his services. After an injury-plagued start at the Etihad, Kalvin made two substitute appearances for England at the 2022 FIFA World Cup. He scored his first international goal in a 7-0 win against North Macedonia in UEFA Euro 2024 qualifying on 19 June 2023.

EBERECHI EZE

Position: Midfielder
Date/Place of Birth: 29 June 1998 - London
England Debut: 16 June 2023 v Malta (A)

Eberechi made his senior England debut in their 4-0 victory over Malta in a UEFA Euro 2024 qualifier on 16 June 2023. The Crystal Palace midfielder's first cap - as a second-half substitute for James Maddison - had been a long time coming, as he was initially called up for the Three Lions' Euro 2020 provisional squad but had to withdraw after getting injured on the same day. Eberechi has been capped at U20 and U21 level for England too and has also trained with the Nigeria national team whom he was eligible to play for due to family connections, but he chose to represent his country of birth.

CONOR GALLAGHER

Position: Midfielder
Date/Place of Birth: 6 February 2000 - Epsom
England Debut: 15 November 2021 v San Marino (A)

At the time of writing, England had lost only one of seven games when Conor was on the pitch while his six other appearances came in victories. The midfielder was having a wonderful season on loan from Chelsea at Crystal Palace when he received his first senior Three Lions call-up and made his debut against San Marino on 15 November 2021. He was included in Gareth Southgate's 2022 FIFA World Cup squad but didn't feature in Qatar. In 2023, Conor collected further caps in UEFA Euro 2024 qualifying victories over Italy, Ukraine and North Macedonia.

FORWARDS

JACK GREALISH

Position: Forward
Date/Place of Birth: 10 September 1995 - Birmingham
England Debut: 8 September 2020 v Denmark (A)

A treble-winner with Manchester City in 2022/23, Jack increased his England caps tally to 32 when he featured in the Three Lions' 7-0 victory over North Macedonia on 19 June 2023 just eight days after winning the UEFA Champions League. The attack-minded player came on as a substitute in all five of England's matches at the 2022 FIFA World Cup. He made two assists in five UEFA 2020 games, setting up Raheem Sterling's winner against Czech Republic and Harry Kane's header against Germany.

CALLUM WILSON

Position: Forward
Date/Place of Birth: 27 February 1992 - Coventry
England Debut: 15 November 2018 v United States (H)

Callum became the first AFC Bournemouth player to score for England when he netted on his international debut against the United States in November 2019. Wilson won four England caps while under contract with the Cherries prior to a 2020 move to Newcastle United. His second England goal came during his seventh England appearance as he netted in the 4-0 win in Malta on 16 June 2023.

HARRY KANE

Position: Forward
Date/Place of Birth: 28 July 1993 - London
England Debut: 27 March 2015 v Lithuania (H)

Breaking Wayne Rooney's record, Harry became England's all-time record scorer when he netted from the penalty spot in a 2-1 win over Italy in Naples on 23 March 2023. The England captain has represented the Three Lions at four major tournaments to date. He scored against Senegal and France at the 2022 FIFA World Cup finals, taking his goal tally at the competition to eight having won the Golden Boot award at the 2018 tournament with six strikes in as many games. He scored four times at UEFA Euro 2020 as England finished tournament runners-up having been the top goal scorer in qualifying with 12 strikes in eight matches.

PHIL FODEN

Position: Forward
Date/Place of Birth: 28 May 2000 - Stockport
England Debut: 5 September 2020 v Iceland (A)

Another of Manchester City's treble-winning class of 2023, Phil has represented England at their last two major tournaments finals. He started in England's 1-0 win over Croatia in their opening match at UEFA Euro 2020 and also featured in two other tournament games. He played in four matches at the 2022 FIFA World Cup, scoring in the 3-0 win against Wales on 29 November 2022. Earlier in his international career, Phil's brace in a 4-0 UEFA Nations League victory over Iceland in November 2020 saw him become the youngest England player ever to score two goals at Wembley Stadium, at the age of 20 years and 174 days.

MARCUS RASHFORD

Position: Forward
Date/Place of Birth: 31 October 1997 - Manchester
England Debut: 27 May 2016 v Australia (H)

Awarded an OBE (Member of the Order of the British Empire) in 2020, Marcus is an inspiring figure on and off the football pitch. At the age of 18 years and 208 days, he became the youngest player ever to score on his England debut in a 2-1 win over Australia in May 2016. Since then, he had been included in England squads for four major tournaments, including the 2022 FIFA World Cup – a competition which saw him score three goals in four appearances. He scored his 16th international goal on the occasion of his 53rd international appearance against North Macedonia in June 2023.

BUKAYO SAKA

Position: Forward
Date/Place of Birth: 5 September 2001 - London
England Debut: 8 October 2020 v Wales (H)

England's Men's Player of the Year for 2021/22, Bukayo scored his first international goal in a 1-0 triumph over Austria prior to representing the Three Lions at UEFA Euro 2020. He was named Man of the Match for his performance against Czech Republic in England's final Group D match at that tournament – one of four fixtures in which he featured during the competition. Bukayo scored twice in England's 6-2 victory over Iran at the 2022 FIFA World Cup and was also on target in the 3-0 win over Senegal at the competition. He scored a hat-trick as England beat North Macedonia 7-0 in June 2023.

RAHEEM STERLING

Position: Forward
Date/Place of Birth: 8 December 1994 - Kingston, Jamaica
England Debut: 14 November 2012 v Sweden (A)

Raheem has played an important role in the England senior squad for more than a decade. By the summer of 2023, Sterling had earnt 82 caps and scored 20 goals for the Three Lions. At the 2022 FIFA World Cup, the winger scored England's third goal in their opening game against Iran. He also featured against the United States and in their quarter-final defeat to France. In addition to the 2022 World Cup, Raheem has played for the Three Lions at the 2014 and 2018 FIFA World Cups and the 2016 and 2020 UEFA European Championships – in the latter he scored three times in seven matches and was included in Team of the Tournament.

LEAH WILLIAMSON

CAPTAIN

ENGLAND SENIOR

6 FIFA WOMEN'S WORLD CUP APPEARANCES

| BEST PERFORMANCE | RUNNERS-UP | 2023 |

BIGGEST WIN

20-0 v LATVIA (H)
30 NOVEMBER 2021

TOP SCORER

52 ELLEN WHITE

WOMEN'S PROFILE

9 UEFA WOMEN'S EUROPEAN CHAMPIONSHIP APPEARANCES

BEST PERFORMANCE   WINNERS   2022

FIRST INTERNATIONAL

3-2 v SCOTLAND (A)

18 NOVEMBER 1972

MOST CAPS

172

SARINA WIEGMAN

HEAD COACH

FARA WILLIAMS

SARINA

TIMELINE

WIEGMAN

1969

Sarina was born in The Hague, Netherlands on 26 October 1969.

1975 / 76

Around the age of six, she played alongside boys at GSC ESDO, before joining her first women's team, HSV Celeritas.

1987

Sarina earned her first senior Netherlands Women call-up at just 16 years of age and made her international debut against Norway on 23 May 1987, while playing for club side KFC '71.

1988

Playing at an international tournament in China in 1988, Sarina met the United States national team manager Anson Dorrance who invited her to play for the North Carolina Tar Heels. During her year at the club, they won the league title and Sarina got to play alongside the likes of US stars Mia Hamm and Kristine Lilly.

1994

On her return to Holland, Wiegman had to find a part-time job which could financially support her footballing exploits. She became a PE teacher at a local school, a job she kept throughout her nine-year stay at Sassenheim based side Ter Leede.

2003

The defensive midfielder won two league titles and one cup while at Ter Leede, eventually hanging up her boots in 2003, two years after she had earned the final of 104 caps for the Dutch national team. FIFA later revealed that five of her caps were against non-FIFA affiliated sides so her official total has now been reduced to 99.

2006

Wiegman started her coaching career in January 2006, leading her former side Ter Leede to a league and cup double the following season - their first silverware for three years.

2007

After a memorable debut season as a manager, Sarina left Ter Leede to take up the top job at ADO Den Haag Women. In a seven-year spell at the club based in The Hague, she lifted one league trophy and two domestic cups.

2014

In August 2014 she became assistant coach with the Netherlands women's national team, working with Roger Reijners and then Arjan van der Laan, with a short spell as interim manager in between.

2016

In October 2016, while still working with the national team, Sarina became assistant manager of the Sparta Rotterdam men's youth team. In doing so she became the first woman to coach in the professional men's game in Holland.

2017

Appointed as head coach of the Dutch women's national team on a permanent basis, Wiegman led them to a stunning title win at UEFA Women's Euro 2017. Her side won every match, including victories over Norway, Sweden and England. She won FIFA Women's Coach of the Year as a result.

2019

In 2019, Wiegman led the Dutch to the World Cup Final but they were beaten 2-0 by eventual champions the United States.

2021

Sarina's first game in charge of the Lionesses was an 8-0 win over North Macedonia in a 2023 World Cup qualifier.

2022

Sarina led the Lionesses to UEFA Women's Euro 2022 glory by beating Germany 2-1 in the final at Wembley Stadium. On the back of their momentous win, Wiegman was named FIFA Women's Coach of the Year for a third time, picked up the BBC Sports Personality of the Year Coach Award and was appointed as an Honorary Commander of the Order of the British Empire (CBE) for services to association football.

2023

More silverware followed in the first half of 2023 as England retained their Arnold Clark Cup title, and the first edition of the Women's Finalissima.

WOMEN'S SENIOR TEAM

PLAYER PROFILES

(H) Home (A) Away (N) Neutral Venue

GOALKEEPERS

MARY EARPS

Position: **Goalkeeper**
Date of Birth: **7 March 1993**
Place of Birth: **Nottingham**
England Debut: **11 June 2017
v Switzerland (A)**

Mary was one of England's standout performers at the 2023 FIFA Women's World Cup – a tournament which saw her claim the Golden Glove award on the back of keeping three clean sheets as the Lionesses progressed to the final. She started all seven matches in Australia and New Zealand and saved a penalty from Spain's Jennifer Hermoso in the final. Her performances in the Southern Hemisphere follow her inspirational showing at UEFA Women's Euro 2022; Mary kept four clean sheets in six matches en route to the Lionesses' famous triumph.

HANNAH HAMPTON

Position: **Goalkeeper**
Date of Birth: **16 November 2000**
Place of Birth: **Birmingham**
England Debut: **20 February 2022
v Spain (N)**

A member of England's squad for both UEFA Women's Euro 2022 and the 2023 FIFA Women's World Cup, Hannah had two caps to her name at the time of writing. The young goalkeeper made her senior international debut during England's successful Arnold Clark Cup campaign. With a shut out on her debut, she went on to keep another clean sheet in their emphatic 10-0 win over North Macedonia in a 2023 FIFA Women's World Cup qualifier in April 2022.

ELLIE ROEBUCK

Position: **Goalkeeper**
Date of Birth: **23 September 1999**
Place of Birth: **Sheffield**
England Debut: **8 November 2018
v Austria (A)**

Like Hannah Hampton, Ellie was named in England's squad for UEFA Women's Euro 2022 and the 2023 FIFA Women's World Cup. The Sheffield-born stopper, who has over 100 Manchester City appearances to her name, had been capped 11 times by the Lionesses at the time of writing, having previously played at U17 and U19 level. She was Great Britain's number one at the delayed 2020 Summer Olympics, where she featured in four matches.

DEFENDERS

MILLIE BRIGHT

Position: Defender
Date of Birth: 21 August 1993
Place of Birth: Chesterfield
England Debut: 20 September 2016
v Belgium (A)

In the absence of Leah Williamson, Millie captained England at the 2023 FIFA Women's World Cup and, along with Mary Earps and Alex Greenwood, played every minute of the tournament. She was an ever-present for the Lionesses at UEFA Women's Euro 2022 too and previously featured in five of England's matches at the 2019 FIFA Women's World Cup, while she was also included in the Team GB squad for the delayed Tokyo Olympic Games in the summer of 2021. Her appearances at the 2023 FIFA Women's World Cup brought her England caps tally to 73.

LUCY BRONZE

Position: Defender
Date of Birth: 28 October 1991
Place of Birth: Berwick-upon-Tweed
England Debut: 26 June 2013
v Japan (H)

One of the finest players of her generation, Lucy has been nominated for the Ballon d'Or Féminin on multiple occasions, finishing runner-up in 2019. A year later, she became the first English player to claim The Best FIFA Women's Player award. The right-back has been included in six major tournament squads for England, dating back to her inclusion in the 23-player squad for UEFA Women's Euro 2013. An-ever present in Sarina Wiegman's starting XI at UEFA Women's Euro 2022 and the 2023 FIFA Women's World Cup, Lucy had brought her Lionesses caps tally to 112 by the end of the latter tournament.

JESS CARTER

Position: Defender
Date of Birth: 27 October 1997
Place of Birth: Warwick
England Debut: 28 November 2017
v Kazakhstan (H)

Jess appeared in England's back three for six of their seven 2023 FIFA Women's World Cup games including for the final against Spain – her 24th match for the Lionesses. The versatile player, who can play in defence or midfield made her senior England debut in 2017, having previously featured at U19, U20 and U21 level. Her first goal for England came in a record-breaking 20-0 victory over Latvia in a 2023 FIFA Women's World Cup qualifier. At club level, she moved from Birmingham City to Chelsea back in 2018.

LEAH WILLIAMSON

Position: Defender/Midfielder
Date of Birth: 29 March 1997
Place of Birth: Milton Keynes
England Debut: 8 June 2018 v Russia (A)

A few weeks after captaining England to success at the 2023 Women's Finalissima, Leah sustained a serious knee injury that ruled her out for the 2023 FIFA Women's World Cup. First handed the England captaincy for a World Cup qualifier against North Macedonia in September 2021, Leah was given the armband permanently in April 2022. Just three months later, she lifted the European Championship trophy for the Lionesses! A commanding presence on the pitch, the Arsenal player had previously turned out for her country in every age group from the U15s to the senior side. of 2021. Her appearances at the 2023 FIFA Women's World Cup brought her England caps tally to 73.

ALEX GREENWOOD

Position: Defender
Date of Birth: 7 September 1993
Place of Birth: Liverpool
England Debut: 5 March 2014
v Italy (N)

Alex played every minute of England's seven matches at the 2023 FIFA Women's World Cup on the back of also appearing in five of the Lionesses' six games on their way to European Championship glory in July 2022. Having previously captained the side for a brief period of England's 20-0 victory over Latvia in November 2021, the Manchester City defender wore the armband from the start in the 2-1 Arnold Cup victory over Italy in Coventry in February 2023. By the end of the 2023 FIFA Women's World Cup, Alex had 82 senior caps and five goals to her name.

NIAMH CHARLES

Position: Defender
Date of Birth: 21 June 1999
Place of Birth: Wirral
England Debut: 9 April 2021
v France (A)

A month after making her senior England debut, right-back Niamh was selected as one of four reserve players for Team GB's squad for the delayed 2020 Summer Olympics. She was also included in the pre-tournament squad for UEFA Women's Euro 2022 but failed to make the final 23. On the back of an excellent season for Chelsea in 2022/23, the Wirral-born player made it into Sarina Wiegman's squad for the 2023 FIFA Women's World Cup, where she made two substitute appearances.

RACHEL DALY

Position: Defender/Forward
Date of Birth: 6 December 1991
Place of Birth: Harrogate
England Debut: 4 June 2016
v Serbia (H)

Rachel demonstrated her versatility at the 2023 Women's World Cup, as she played at left-wing-back and left midfield during the competition. She has also previously played up front for the Lionesses. Wearing the number 9 shirt during the competition, Rachel netted in England's 6-1 Group D thrashing of China – her 14th international goal. The Harrogate-born player appeared in all seven of the Lionesses matches in Australia and New Zealand – six as a starter – while she started all six matches at UEFA Women's Euro 2022.

LOTTE WUBBEN-MOY

Position: Defender
Date of Birth: 11 January 1999
Place of Birth: London
England Debut: 23 February 2021
v Northern Ireland (H)

Lotte was an unused substitute for England's victory over Brazil in the 2023 Women's Finalissima. She was also on the bench for each of the Lionesses' matches at the 2023 FIFA Women's World Cup but was one of six non-playing members of Sarina Wiegman's squad at the tournament. Lotte captained England U17s at the 2016 FIFA U17 Women's World Cup, leading them to the quarter-finals. By the start of the 2023 FIFA Women's World Cup, she had played 10 senior matches for England having also previously turned out at U15, U20 and U21 level.

ESME MORGAN

Position: Defender
Date of Birth: 18 October 2000
Place of Birth: Sheffield
England Debut: 12 October 2022 v Czech Republic (H)

Esme became a regular for Manchester City during the 2022/23 season, featuring in 23 matches in all competitions. Her form for Gareth Taylor's side saw her included in the Lionesses' squad for the 2023 FIFA Women's World Cup. By the start of the tournament, the lifelong City supporter had five caps to her name having previously featured for the Young Lionesses at U17, U19 and U21 level.

MIDFIELDERS

JORDAN NOBBS

Position: Midfielder
Date of Birth: 8 December 1992
Place of Birth: Stockton-on-Tees
England Debut: 6 March 2013
v Italy (N)

Jordan has been a mainstay of the England squad since making her debut for the Lionesses back in 2013. The midfielder, who previously appeared for the Young Lionesses at U17, U19, U20 and U23 level, had won 71 caps for the senior side by the end of the 2023 FIFA World Cup – the fourth major tournament squad she was included in after UEFA Women's Euro 2013 and 2019 and the 2015 FIFA Women's World Cup. A former Sunderland and Arsenal player, Jordan signed for BWSL side Aston Villa in 2023.

KEIRA WALSH

Position: Midfielder
Date of Birth: 8 April 1997
Place of Birth: Rochdale
England Debut: 28 November 2017 v Kazakhstan (H)

Keira featured in six out of England's seven matches at the 2023 FIFA Women's World Cup, which brought her senior caps tally to 65. Earlier in the year, she started in the victory over Brazil in the 2023 Women's Finalissima. Keira's performance in the UEFA Women's Euro 2022 final against Germany – which included her setting up Ella Toone's opening goal - saw her named Player of the Match. She started all six games at the tournament for Sarina Wiegman's side and sealed a move from Manchester City to Barcelona later that year.

LAURA COOMBS

Position: Midfield
Date of Birth: 29 January 1991
Place of Birth: Gravesend
England Debut: 23 October 2015
v China (A)

Having not played for England since 2015, Laura returned to the Lionesses' fold for the 2023 Arnold Clark Cup. She came on as a substitute for Georgia Stanway in the 4-0 victory over South Korea and then started in the 2-1 triumph over Italy in the competition. She made two substitute appearances at the 2023 FIFA Women's World Cup which brought her international cap tally to seven.

GEORGIA STANWAY

Position: Midfielder
Date of Birth: 3 January 1999
Place of Birth: Barrow-in-Furness
England Debut: 8 November 2018 v Austria (A)

Georgia's penalty gave England a 1-0 victory over Haiti in the Lionesses' first match of the 2023 FIFA Women's World Cup. It was her second international goal of the year and 16th overall and came during a year in which she collected her 50th England cap. A winner of the PFA Women's Young Player of the Year back in 2018/19, the Cumbrian has developed into one of the finest midfielders in world football. She won the Frauen-Bundesliga with Bayern Munich in 2022/23 having previously won seven major trophies at her previous club, Manchester City.

KATIE ZELEM

Position: Midfielder
Date of Birth: 20 January 1996
Place of Birth: Oldham
England debut: 30 November 2021 v Latvia (H)

Katie replaced Keira Walsh as a substitute in England's record 20-0 victory over Latvia in November 2021 to make her senior international debut. Capped between U15 and U23 level, Katie represented England at the FIFA U20 World Cup in Canada in 2014 and helped the U19s to a second-place finish at the UEFA Women's U19 Euro finals the year before that. She made two appearances at the 2023 FIFA Women's World Cup, as a starter against China and from the bench against Nigeria.

ELLA TOONE

Position: Midfielder
Date of Birth: 2 September 1999
Place of Birth: Tyldesley
England Debut: 23 February 2021 v Northern Ireland (H)

Ella has scored some important goals for England in recent years, registering in the 2023 Women's Finalissima against Brazil while she got the opener in a 3-1 victory over Australia in the 2023 FIFA Women's World Cup semi-final. She also netted twice at UEFA Women's Euro 2022 - an 84th minute equaliser against Spain in the quarter-finals to send the game into extra-time and the opener in the final against Germany. By the end of the 2023 FIFA Women's World Cup, the attack-minded midfielder had scored 17 goals in 38 England appearances.

FORWARDS

BETHANY ENGLAND

Position: Forward
Date of Birth: 3 June 1994
Place of Birth: Barnsley
England Debut: 29 August 2019 v Belgium (A)

Bethany moved across London in January 2023 to sign for Tottenham Hotspur for a reported British record transfer fee of £250,000. The forward settled into her new surroundings quickly, scoring 13 goals in 14 Spurs appearances in the second half of the 2022/23 season. Her form in front of goal was rewarded with a place in Sarina Wiegman's 23-player squad for the 2023 FIFA Women's World Cup. She made five substitute appearances during the tournament bringing her caps tally to 26.

LAUREN HEMP

Position: Forward
Date of Birth: 7 August 2000
Place of Birth: North Walsham
England Debut: 8 October 2019 v Portugal (A)

Lauren scored three goals in seven appearances at the 2023 FIFA Women's World Cup, with strikes against China in the group stage and Colombia and Australia in the knockout phase. She also provided the assist for Alessia Russo's goal in the 3-1 semi-final win over Australia. A year earlier, Lauren started every game as the Lionesses triumphed at UEFA Euro 2022 and scored in the 8-0 thumping of Norway in the group stage. She also started in the 2023 Women's Finalissima.

CHLOE KELLY

Position: Forward
Date of Birth: 15 January 1998
Place of Birth: London
England Debut: 8 November 2018 v Austria (A)

Chloe etched her name into English footballing folklore, coming off the bench to score the Lionesses' winning goal in the 2-1 extra-time victory over Germany in the final of UEFA Women's Euro 2022. Head Coach Sarina Wiegman looked to the London-born forward to repeat her 'super sub' heroics at the 2023 FIFA Women's World Cup, with five of Chloe's seven appearances at the tournament coming from the bench. As well netting in the UEFA Women's Euro 2022 Final, Chloe scored the winning spot-kick in England's 4-2 penalty shootout victory against Brazil in the 2023 Women's Finalissima.

BETH MEAD

Position: Forward
Date of Birth: 9 May 1995
Place of Birth: Whitby
England Debut: 6 April 2018 v Wales (H)

Beth suffered the heartbreak of missing out on the 2023 FIFA Women's World Cup having ruptured her anterior cruciate ligament playing for Arsenal against Manchester United in November 2022. At UEFA Women's Euro 2022, Beth picked up the 'Golden Boot' award having bagged six goals en route to winning the tournament with the Lionesses. As of August 2023, she had scored 29 goals in 50 appearances for England.

ALESSIA RUSSO

Position: Forward
Date of Birth: 8 February 1999
Place of Birth: Maidstone
England Debut: 11 March 2020 v Spain (N)

Alessia started all seven of England's matches at the 2023 FIFA Women's World Cup and scored three goals at the competition – including the third in the 3-1 win over Australia in the semi-final which brought her Lionesses tally to 14 strikes in 28 appearances. A year earlier, her audacious back-heel in England's UEFA Women's Euro 2022 semi-final victory over Sweden earnt the striker the 'Goal of the Tournament' award. Alessia scored her first England goals with a hat-trick against Latvia during the Lionesses' record 20-0 win in November 2021.

LAUREN JAMES

Position: Forward
Date of Birth: 29 September 2001
Place of Birth: London
England Debut: 3 September 2022 v Austria (A)

Lauren was England's most productive player at the 2023 Women's World Cup in terms of goal involvement as she netted three times and made three assists. Two of those goals and all three assists came against China while she also got the Lionesses' winner against Denmark. She made five appearances in the tournament altogether, playing in all three group games plus the round of 16 match against Nigeria and the final against Spain, which saw her introduced as a half-time substitute.

KATIE ROBINSON

Position: Forward
Date of Birth: 8 August 2022
Place of Birth: Cornwall
England Debut: 15 November 2022 v Norway (N)

Katie was England's youngest member of Sarina Wiegman's 23-player squad for the 2023 FIFA Women's World Cup with the forward celebrating her 21st birthday during the tournament. Previously capped at U17 level, the Brighton & Hove Albion forward had five senior caps to her name prior to the World Cup. She was introduced as a late substitute in the 2023 Women's Finalissima but didn't feature at the World Cup.

CROSSWORD

Add the surnames of these current England Men's Senior players to complete this crossword.

ACROSS

2. Centre-back who earned his first senior England cap in a 6-0 win away to Bulgaria in October 2019 - TYRONE _ _ _ _ _ (5)

4. His £30m move to Manchester United from Southampton in 2014 was a then-world record transfer fee for a teenager - LUKE _ _ _ _ (4)

6. Won the FA Cup and FA Community Shield with Leicester City in 2021 - JAMES _ _ _ _ _ _ _ _ (8)

8. Striker who finished the 2022/23 season as Newcastle United's top scorer - CALLUM _ _ _ _ _ _ (6)

10. The Three Lions' all-time record goalscorer - HARRY _ _ _ _ (4)

11. Full-back who started his career at boyhood club Sheffield United before moving to Tottenham Hotspur - KYLE _ _ _ _ _ _ (6)

12. Scored on his England debut in a 2-1 friendly victory over Australia in May 2016 - MARCUS _ _ _ _ _ _ _ _ (8)

DOWN

1. Captained West Ham United to UEFA Europa Conference League glory in 2022/23 - DECLAN _ _ _ _ (4)

3. Winger who won back-to-back Player of the Season awards at Arsenal in 2020/21 and 2021/22 - BUKAYO _ _ _ _ (4)

5. Midfielder who joined Liverpool in June 2011 and went on to captain the side - JORDAN _ _ _ _ _ _ _ _ _ (9)

7. Goalkeeper who picked up his 50th cap in England's quarter-final defeat to France at the 2022 FIFA World Cup - JORDAN _ _ _ _ _ _ _ _ (8)

9. Won the treble with Manchester City in 2022/23 after joining the club from Aston Villa in 2021 - JACK _ _ _ _ _ _ _ _ (8)

Answers on pages 60-61

WORDSEARCH

Find the surnames of 10 different members of England's 2023 FIFA Women's World Cup squad.

T	G	R	E	E	N	W	O	O	D	R	E	O	A
A	L	E	R	S	W	G	Y	T	O	W	A	T	E
S	O	A	K	E	L	L	Y	S	W	E	R	E	N
A	S	W	R	T	H	G	I	R	B	N	M	H	G
S	R	U	S	S	O	N	S	W	A	L	S	H	L
T	B	E	Y	H	O	C	O	O	M	B	S	C	A
O	E	O	G	H	L	T	O	E	G	W	M	S	N
T	E	Y	S	L	T	W	O	S	N	O	O	L	D
S	L	A	N	W	Y	A	W	T	O	O	A	N	O
S	D	S	R	O	C	A	N	A	O	A	T	E	S
S	G	N	N	P	E	G	G	N	T	O	O	N	E
L	O	H	W	S	S	A	A	W	E	R	Y	D	O
W	A	A	B	T	G	G	P	A	O	L	T	T	T
O	D	S	D	E	W	A	S	Y	S	R	D	I	S

Answers on pages 60-61

BRIGHT   **EARPS**   **GREENWOOD**   **RUSSO**   **TOONE**
COOMBS   **ENGLAND**   **KELLY**   **STANWAY**   **WALSH**

RECORD BREAKER!

Harry Kane became England's record goalscorer in March 2023 as he bagged his 54th senior goal for the Three Lions in a 2-1 win against Italy in Naples. Let's take a look back at some of Kane's landmark goals for the Three Lions.

GOAL 1

ENGLAND 4 LITHUANIA 0

UEFA Euro 2016 Qualifying
27 March 2015
Wembley Stadium

Just 80 seconds after coming on as a substitute for Wayne Rooney to make his senior international debut, Harry scored his first England goal as he headed home from a Raheem Sterling cross.

GOAL 4

ENGLAND 3 GERMANY 2

Friendly
26 March 2016
Olympiastadion Berlin

Harry's goal on 61 minutes kick-started England's impressive comeback against the World Cup holders. The Three Lions were trailing 2-0 when he scored with a low, well-placed strike - his first international goal as an England starter.

GOALS 14-19
2018 FIFA WORLD CUP

Kane claimed the Golden Boot award at the 2018 FIFA World Cup with six strikes in the tournament in Russia. He got an important brace in England's Group G opener against Tunisia on 18 June 2018 as he gave the Three Lions the lead on 11 minutes

before scoring their winner in stoppage time at the end of the 90 minutes with a header.

Six days later Harry scored his first senior England hat-trick in a 6-1 win over Panama. He coolly converted two penalties in the first half before a fortunate deflection from Ruben Loftus-Cheek's effort completed his treble.
Kane was called upon to put the Three Lions ahead in their round of 16 tie against Colombia and he made no mistake from the penalty spot on 57 minutes after being brought down in the area. Colombia equalised to take the game into extra-time and a penalty shootout, which England won for the first time ever, with Kane one of the players on target.

GOALS 23-25
ENGLAND 4 BULGARIA 0

UEFA Euro 2020 Qualifying
7 September 2019
Wembley Stadium

The England captain opened the scoring at Wembley as he finished from close range while on the turn, following a lovely pass from Raheem Sterling. Harry's second and third goals of the day both came from the penalty spot again, as he completed his second senior international hat-trick to surpass the great Sir Geoff Hurst's scoring tally of 24 goals for England.

GOALS 29-31
ENGLAND 7 MONTENEGRO 0

UEFA Euro 2020 Qualifying
14 November 2019
Wembley Stadium

England's 1,000th match saw them secure qualification for UEFA Euro 2020 and Harry was on the scoresheet once again. The Three Lions' captain scored a superb hat-trick - including two headers - in just 19 first-half minutes to become the first English player to score a treble in consecutive games at Wembley.

GOALS 35-38
UEFA EURO 2020

At the delayed UEFA Euro 2020, Harry's knack of scoring against Germany continued with a stooping header in the 86th-minute of England's round of 16 tie to secure a 2-0 victory on 29 June 2021, and a quarter-final meeting with Ukraine.

The England captain had his shooting boots on again four days later as it took him just four minutes to find the back of the net at Stadio Olimpico in Rome after a well-timed through ball from Raheem Sterling. Harry's second of the night came when he headed home from a Luke Shaw Cross to help England to a 4-0 win.

Kane was the hero at Wembley on 7 July 2021 when his 104th-minute winner against Denmark booked England a place in the Euro 2020 final. The referee pointed to the penalty spot after Raheem Sterling was fouled in the area, and despite Sweden 'keeper Kasper Schmeichel saving Harry's initial effort, the rebound fell to him and he buried the ball in the back of the net.

GOALS 42-44
ENGLAND 5 ALBANIA 0

2022 FIFA World Cup Qualifying
12 November 2021
Wembley Stadium

The last England player to get a 'perfect hat-trick' - when you score with both feet and your head - was David Platt in February 1993. So, Harry's first-half treble against Albania was certainly another one for the history books.

He headed home from Jordan Henderson's cross on 18 minutes before firing into the far top corner with his left foot to make it 4-0 just after the half-hour mark. An acrobatic, right-footed volley from Ben Chilwell's corner in extra-time at the end of the first 45 completed Harry's hat-trick and the Three Lions' rout.

GOALS 45-48
ENGLAND 10
SAN MARINO 0

2022 FIFA World Cup Qualifying
15 November 2021
San Marino Stadium

The Three Lions skipper proved he is just as comfortable scoring on the road as he is at home with an impressive goalscoring display at San Marino. Just three days after his hat-trick against Albania, Harry added another four goals to his tally.

He showed his ruthlessness from the penalty spot once again to open his account for England's third of the night, and made it a brace just four minutes later, this time from open play. Another converted penalty gave him his hat-trick to make it five for the Three Lions, before some quick footwork saw Kane dazzle the San Marino defence and he finished in the far corner – all four of his goals coming before the break.

GOAL 54
ENGLAND 2
ITALY 1

UEFA Euro 2024 Qualifying
23 March 2023
Stadio Diego Armando Maradona

Harry's record-breaking 54th England goal came from the penalty spot as the Three Lions captain sent Italy 'keeper Gianluigi Donnarumma the wrong way to double their lead in Naples.

WOMEN'S FINALISSIMA

The Lionesses took on Brazil in the first ever Women's Finalissima, which pitched the current European Champions against the victors of the Women's Copa America – South America's major continental tournament.

On April 6 2023 a crowd of more than 83,000 at Wembley Stadium saw Sarina Wiegman's side go ahead through Ella Toone after she rifled home from a Lucy Bronze cut back on 23 minutes.

ENGLAND

Earps, Bronze, Carter, Walsh, Williamson, Greenwood, James (Kelly 74), Stanway, Russo (Daly 74), Toone, Hemp (Robinson 88)

BRAZIL

Leticia, Antonia (Gabi Nunes 87), Lauren (Andressa Alves 46), Kathellen, Rafaelle, Tamires, Luana (Duda Francelino 69), Ary Borges (Fernanda 87), Kerolin, Bia Zaneratto (Adriana 46), Geyse Ferreira

England thought they had doubled their lead shortly after but Lauren James' 'goal' was flagged for offside. Lauren Hemp and Alessia Russo also had efforts late on in the first half.

After the break, England 'keeper Mary Earps made a stunning save from Geyse's long-range shot, and Georgia Stanway and substitute Rachel Daly both came close for the Lionesses but they couldn't find the all-important second goal.

Three minutes into stoppage time Andressa Alves equalised for Brazil from close range to take the game to penalties – the first shootout Wiegman's side has encountered.

But Stanway, Daly, Alex Greenwood and Chloe Kelly all confidently scored their spot kicks as England triumphed 4-2 on penalties to add the Finalissima trophy to their silverware cabinet.

ENGLAND QUIZ

TEST YOUR KNOWLEDGE WITH 30 QUESTIONS ON ENGLAND TEAMS THROUGH THE AGES...

1) What year did the Three Lions win the FIFA World Cup for the first (and, to date, only) time?

2) What European competition did Declan Rice win with West Ham United in 2023?

3) How many steps are there from pitch level to the Royal Box at Wembley Stadium?

4) How many teams will compete at UEFA Euro 2024?

5) Against which nation did Gareth Southgate make his senior debut as an England player?

6) What year did England host the European Championships?

7) Who were England opponents in the UEFA Euro 2020 Final?

8) Which club did Bethany England sign for in January 2023 for a reported record British transfer fee?

9) Who was appointed the Lionesses' captain for the 2023 FIFA Women's World Cup in the absence of Leah Williamson?

10) Which nation were opponents for both the Three Lions and the Lionesses in their first international matches in 1872 and 1972 respectively?

11) In what showpiece match did the Lionesses face Brazil at Wembley Stadium on 6 April 2023?

12) Who scored two goals for England in their 3-0 win over Wales at the 2022 FIFA World Cup?

13) In which city was Jack Grealish born on 10 September 1995?

14) Which country did England play their group matches at 2023 FIFA Women's World Cup?

15) Who did England face in their first match at the 2023 FIFA Women's World Cup?

16) What group were England in at the 2023 FIFA Women's World Cup?

17) How many FIFA World Cup tournaments have the Three Lions appeared at to date?

18) Which Spanish club did Jude Bellingham sign for on 1 June 2023?

19) Who was the head coach of England's Under-20 side at the 2023 FIFA U-20 World Cup?

20) Which nation eliminated England from the 2023 UEFA Women's Under-17 Championships?

21) In which city was Mary Earps born on 7 March 1993?

22) Who did England Cerebral Palsy face in the 2023 IFCPF European Championship final?

23) Which England CP stopper was named Best Goalkeeper at the 2023 IFCPF European Championships?

24) Who was the captain of the England team that won the 1966 FIFA World Cup?

25) With which FA Women's Super League side did Katie Robinson start her professional career?

26) Who was named England Men's Player of the Year for 2021/22?

27) Who was named England Women's Player of the Year for 2021/22?

28) How many senior England goals had Harry Kane scored when he netted with a penalty against Italy in March 2023?

29) In which country was Sarina Wiegman born on 26 October 1969?

30) What year did the Lionesses win the UEFA Women's European Championships for the first (and, to date, only) time?

Answers on page 60-61

CHAMPIONS!

Lee Carsley's Young Lions were victorious at the UEFA Under-21 2023 – England's first triumph at the competition since 1984.

England were one of 16 teams that took part in the tournament which was hosted by Romania and Georgia between 21 June and 8 July 2023. The Young Lions topped Group C with wins over Czechia, Israel and Germany before seeing off Portugal and Israel again in the knockout phase en route to a final meeting with Spain. A 1-0 victory over their Spanish counterparts saw England U21s enter the record books as the first team to win the tournament without conceding a single goal.

GROUP PHASE

CZECHIA 0 ENGLAND 2

UEFA UNDER-21 EURO 2023 · GROUP C
22 JUNE 2023
ADJARABET ARENA, BATUMI

ENGLAND LINE-UP: Trafford, Aarons (Johnson 88), Colwill, Harwood-Bellis, Garner, Gibbs-White (Elliott 88), Ramsey, Jones, Gomes (Skipp 79), Gordon (Archer 79), Madueke (Smith Rowe 79)

England got off to the perfect start at Under-21 Euro 2023 with a 2-0 win over Czechia in Group C. Aston Villa's Jacob Ramsey slotted home their opener two minutes into the second half before Arsenal midfielder Emile Smith Rowe finished from close range late in stoppage time to seal victory for the Young Lions.

ENGLAND 2 ISRAEL 0

UEFA UNDER-21 EURO 2023 · GROUP C
25 JUNE 2023
RAMAZ SHENGELIA STADIUM, KUTAISI

ENGLAND LINE-UP: Trafford, Johnson, Harwood-Bellis, Colwill, Garner, Gibbs-White (Ramsey 79), Gomes (Skipp 70), Jones, Smith Rowe (Elliott 70), Madueke (Palmer 61), Gordon (Archer 61)

Another fine display by England's youngsters saw them beat Israel 2-0 to secure top spot in Group C and a place in the knockout phase of the tournament. Morgan Gibbs-White's cross found Anthony Gordon who headed in on 15 minutes to open the scoring and it was the Nottingham Forest midfielder who set up Smith Rowe for the Young Lions' second as well, midway through the second half.

ENGLAND 2 GERMANY 0

ENGLAND LINE-UP: Trafford, Thomas, Braithwaite, Cresswell, Johnson (Aarons 59), Skipp, Palmer, Ramsey (Smith Rowe 59), Elliott, Madueke (Garner 59), Archer (Gordon 69)

Lee Carsley's Young Lions completed their trio of group games with another 2-0 victory – this time over defending champions Germany. England went ahead through Aston Villa striker Cameron Archer after just four minutes and Liverpool's Harvey Elliott doubled their advantage with a lovely solo effort, running from the halfway line and beating his man before powering a shot into the bottom corner on 21 minutes.

FINAL GROUP C TABLE

	P	W	D	L	GF	GA	GD	PTS
1 England (Q)	3	3	0	0	6	0	+6	9
2 Israel (Q)	3	1	1	1	2	3	-1	6
3 Czechia	3	1	0	2	2	4	-2	3
4 Germany	3	0	1	2	2	5	-3	1

KNOCKOUT PHASE

ENGLAND 1 PORTUGAL 0

ENGLAND LINE-UP: Trafford, Aarons (Johnson 74), Colwill, Harwood-Bellis, Garner, Ramsey (Smith Rowe 67), Jones, Gomes (Skipp 80), Madueke (Palmer), Gibbs-White, Gordon

Anthony Gordon scored his second goal of the tournament to give England a 1-0 victory over Portugal in their European U21 Championship quarter-final. The Newcastle striker finished from inside the area just after the half-hour mark to see the Young Lions through to a semi-final clash with Israel, having yet to concede a goal in the tournament.

ISRAEL 0 ENGLAND 3

ENGLAND LINE-UP: Trafford, Thomas, Colwill, Harwood-Bellis, Garner, Smith Rowe (Elliott 74), Jones (Doyle 88), Gomes (Skipp 79), Palmer, Gordon (Archer 74), Gibbs-White (Madueke 79)

England U21s put three past Israel with no reply to book their place in the final of Euro 23. Morgan Gibbs-White made up for an earlier penalty miss when he headed home three minutes before the break in their semi-final tie. The Young Lions doubled their lead just after the hour mark when Manchester City's Cole Palmer finished at the far post and substitute Cameron Archer got England's third in the 90th minute. The result sees England U21s reach a European final for the first time since 2009.

ENGLAND 1 SPAIN 0

ENGLAND LINE-UP: Trafford, Aarons, Colwill, Harwood-Bellis, Garner, Smith Rowe (Madueke 67), Jones, Gomes (Skipp 73), Palmer (Elliott 83), Gordon (Doyle 83), Gibbs-White (Archer 73)

A last-minute penalty save from England U21s 'keeper James Trafford against Spain saw the Young Lions lift their first U21 European Championship title in 39 years. Lee Carsley's side went ahead on the stroke of half-time when Cole Palmer's free-kick deflected off Curtis Jones and into the net. Spain had a 'goal' ruled out for offside in the second half before a late, lengthy VAR check judged Abel Ruiz had been fouled by Chelsea's Levi Colwill in the box. In the 99th minute, Trafford saved the resulting spot kick, and an immediate follow-up effort, to seal victory for England.

2023 MEN'S U-20 WORLD CUP

Ian Foster's England Under-20s competed in the 24-team FIFA U-20 World Cup in the summer of 2023, which took place in Argentina between 20 May and 11 June. Having previously won the competition in 2017, the Young Lions topped their group table in South America before suffering elimination to eventual tournament runners-up Italy in the round of 16.

GROUP PHASE

ENGLAND 1 TUNISIA 0

FIFA U-20 World Cup - Group E
22 May 2023
Estadio Único Diego
Armando Maradona, La Plata

Dane Scarlett scored the only goal of the game as England made a winning start to their U-20 World Cup campaign. The Tottenham Hotspur forward headed home midway through the first half in a game where the Young Lions dominated possession.

ENGLAND LINE-UP: Cox, Scott, Humphreys (Simons 75), Quansah, Devine, Scarlett (Jebbison 81), Vale, Gyabi, Edwards, Edozie (Joseph 75), Oyegoke

URUGUAY 2 ENGLAND 3

FIFA U-20 World Cup - Group E
25 May 2023
Estadio Único Diego Armando Maradona, La Plata

England led 2-0 at half-time thanks to goals from Bashir Humphreys and Alfie Devine in a fiercely contested tie against eventual Champions Uruguay. La Celeste pulled one back shortly after the interval through Franco González but Darko Gyabi restored the Three Lions' two-goal cushion in stoppage time. Matías Abaldo hit the target in the final moments of the game but England held on for the win.

ENGLAND LINE-UP: Cox, Norton-Cuffy (Oyegoke 62), Scott, Humphreys (Doyle 90+8), Quansah (Delap 90+7), Devine, Scarlett, Chukwuemeka, Vale (Edozie 90+8), Edwards, Joseph (Gyabi 62)

IRAQ 0 ENGLAND 0

FIFA U-20 World Cup - Group E
28 May 2023
Estadio Único Diego Armando Maradona, La Plata

England U-20s finished top of Group E to progress to the knockout phase of the World Cup. Sam Edozie had a 'goal' ruled out for offside and Liam Delap had a penalty saved late on in the first half as England were forced to settle for a point against Iraq in their final group game.

ENGLAND LINE-UP: Beadle (Sharman-Lowe 45), Humphreys, Quansah, Devine, Simons, Vale, Edwards, Hines-Samuels (Gyabi 61), Edozie (Scarlett 81), Delap (Jebbison 69), Oyegokev

FINAL GROUP E TABLE

	P	W	D	L	GF	GA	GD	PTS
1 England (Q)	3	2	1	0	4	2	+2	7
2 Uruguay (Q)	3	2	0	1	7	3	+4	6
3 Tunisia (Q)	3	1	0	2	3	2	+1	3
4 Iraq	3	0	1	2	0	7	−7	1

KNOCKOUT PHASE

ENGLAND 1 ITALY 2

FIFA U-20 World Cup - Round of 16
31 May 2023
Estadio Único Diego Armando Maradona, La Plata

The Young Lions bowed out of the World Cup at the hands of Italy who scored a late penalty in their round of 16 tie to win 2-1. Alfie Devine's first half volley cancelled out Italy's early opener courtesy of Tommaso Baldanzi, and though England had chances to take the lead they couldn't capitalise and Cesare Casadei despatched the winning spot-kick with eight minutes of the 90 remaining.

ENGLAND LINE-UP: Cox, Norton-Cuffy (Oyegoke 62), Scott, Humphreys (Doyle 90+8), Quansah (Delap 90+7), Devine, Scarlett, Chukwuemeka, Vale (Edozie 90+8), Edwards, Joseph (Gyabi 62)

2023 UEFA MEN'S U-17 CHAMPIONSHIP

England were one of 16 teams who competed in the UEFA Under-17 Championship, which was staged in Hungary between 17 May and 2 June 2023. Germany overcame France on penalties in the final to lift the trophy as the Young Lions made their first appearance at the tournament since 2019.

England got off to a winning start in their opening Group D game on 18 May 2023, beating Croatia 1-0 thanks to an Ethan Nwaneri goal after just eight minutes. They picked up a further three points in their second fixture three days later, defeating the Netherlands 4-1. A brace by Isaiah Dada-Mascoll and goals from Myles Lewis-Skelly and Justin Oboavwoduo saw Ryan Garry's side complete a comfortable victory.

Qualification for the quarter-finals was secured as England drew 0-0 with Switzerland in their final Group D fixture. It gave the Young Lions an all-important point and they topped their group on goal difference.

Holders France were their opponents in the quarter-finals at Balmazújváros Városi Stadion on 27 May 2023. It was a hard-fought affair with the French finally breaking the deadlock in the 89th minute as Mathis Lambourde's converted spot kick proved the difference between the two sides.

That defeat wasn't the last of England's matches though. As one of the two best losing quarter-finalists, they took on Switzerland in a play-off for the chance to qualify for the FIFA U-17 World Cup.

Archie Gray opened the scoring for England after 17 minutes before the Swiss went ahead with two goals either side of half-time. But Garry's team fought back with a trio of goals from Zakariya Lovelace, Michael Golding and Kadan Young within nine second-half minutes, to win 4-2 and clinch the U-17 World Cup spot.

Photo by Hungarian Football Federation.

2023 UEFA WOMEN'S U-17 CHAMPIONSHIP!

The Young Lionesses reached the semi-finals of the UEFA Women's Under-17 Championship. Eight teams competed in the tournament which was staged in Estonia between 14-26 May 2023.

With head coach Natalie Henderson unable to travel to the tournament due to personal reasons, experienced coach Mo Marley took charge of the Young Lionesses for the 2023 UEFA Women's Under-17 Championships. England defeated Poland 2-1 in their opening Group B game on 14 May 2023. Michelle Agyemang opened the scoring for the Young Lionesses after just four minutes, before bagging her second midway through the first half. Poland pulled one back in stoppage time through Wiktoria Kuprowska but it was a mere consolation.

Agyemang was on target again in England's second fixture against Sweden. This time it took the forward 12 minutes to find the net but a Katie Reid own goal saw the two sides go in level at the break. Marley's team made a confident start to the second half and Agyemang chipped the ball past Sweden's goalkeeper Julia Cavander on 49 minutes to take the lead once more. Ava Baker produced a lovely curling shot for England's third.

The Young Lionesses finished as Group B runners-up on goal difference following a 1-1 draw with France in their final group game. Mari Ward's long-distance effort flew past France 'keeper Lou Marchal to give England the lead just before half-time but Chancelle Effa Effa equalised for the French with 25 minutes to go as they topped the group.

England suffered heartbreak late on in their semi-final against Spain as the reigning world champions scored twice in the final minutes to book their place in the final. The game looked like it was going to penalties after Spain's early opener from Vicky López was cancelled out by Katie Reid's header on 55 minutes. But the Spaniards scored in the 88th minute (Ainoa Gómez) and first minute of stoppage time (Pau) to win 3-1 and knock the Young Lionesses out of the tournament.

France beat Spain 3-2 in the final of the competition to lift the trophy for the first time.

2023 ROUND-UP

A look back on the past year for other England teams.

WOMEN'S U23S

Mo Marley's WU23s played two friendly matches in the space of four days in February 2023. After a goalless draw with Spain at St George's Park, the Young Lionesses produced an impressive performance to beat Belgium 4-1 at Tranmere Rovers' Prenton Park ground. Missy Bo Kearns opened the scoring in the match before Marie Minnaert levelled for the visitors 11 minutes later. After the break, goals from Angela Addison, Anna Patten and Kiera Skeels sealed a comfortable victory.

England twice came from behind to win 3-2 against Portugal in Marinha Grande in April 2023. Jassie Vasconcelos gave the Seleção the lead early on and also netted soon after Addison's second half leveller for the Young Lionesses. However, an 85th-minute equaliser from Laura Blindkilde and a stoppage time winner from Bo Kearns gave the visitors a memorable win at Estádio Municipal da Marinha Grande.

The WU23s extended their run of unbeaten matches - which began with a 1-1 draw in Sweden on 10 October 2022 – to seven with a goalless draw with Belgium in Genk in April 2023. A penalty shootout took place at the end of the game at the Cegeka Arena, with Anna Patten, Aggie Beever-Jones, Laura Brown, Freya Gregory and Molly Pike all scoring as the Young Lionesses triumphed 5-4 on spot-kicks.

WOMEN'S U19S

Amy Merricks became WU19s head coach in April 2023 - the same month the team competed in three UEFA Women's U19 Championship qualification round two matches. A stoppage time Katy Watson goal gave England a 1-1 draw against Slovenia in their opening Group A4 match.

A 5-2 victory over Belarus – which featured braces from Freya Godfrey and Alex Hennessy and a further strike from Lucia Kendall meant the Young Lionesses could qualify for the tournament IF they beat Spain in their final Group A4 match. Alas, it was Spain who triumphed 1-0 in the match in Nyon, Switzerland.

CEREBRAL PALSY

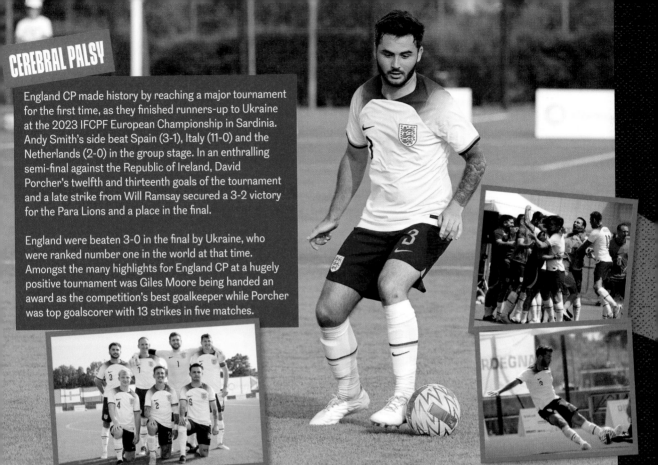

England CP made history by reaching a major tournament for the first time, as they finished runners-up to Ukraine at the 2023 IFCPF European Championship in Sardinia. Andy Smith's side beat Spain (3-1), Italy (11-0) and the Netherlands (2-0) in the group stage. In an enthralling semi-final against the Republic of Ireland, David Porcher's twelfth and thirteenth goals of the tournament and a late strike from Will Ramsay secured a 3-2 victory for the Para Lions and a place in the final.

England were beaten 3-0 in the final by Ukraine, who were ranked number one in the world at that time. Amongst the many highlights for England CP at a hugely positive tournament was Giles Moore being handed an award as the competition's best goalkeeper while Porcher was top goalscorer with 13 strikes in five matches.

MEN'S U19S

England MU19s were unable to secure qualification to the 2023 UEFA U19 Championships, despite having won the competition a year earlier.

With only eight places at the tournament finals available, Simon Rusk's team made it through to the final round of qualifying – known as the elite round. Placed in a four-team group with Iceland, Turkey and Hungary, only the nation finishing top of the group would advance to the finals. Things started well for the Young Lions as a goal from Charlie Webster saw them beat Hungary 1-0 in their first group game in Walsall on 22 March 2023. But a 1-0 defeat to Iceland in Rotherham three days later proved decisive. A 2-0 win over Turkey in Chesterfield was not enough for Rusk's side as Iceland beat Hungary 2-0 that same night to top the group while England finished second.

MEN'S U18S

England MU18s ended the 2022/23 season competing in the International Tournament of Lisbon in June 2023. On the occasion of his 18th birthday, Rio Kyerematen scored in a 2-2 draw with Norway on 9 June 2023 in the Young Lions' first match at the tournament. Romain Esse also scored for Neil Ryan's team in that game.

A brace from Zach Marsh and late winner from Adrian Blake gave England a 3-2 victory against Australia before a goalless draw with hosts Portugal four days later ensured the Young Lions claimed the International Tournament of Lisbon trophy.

GUESS THE GOALSCORER

1.

Who wrapped up England's 4-2 extra-time victory over West Germany in the 1966 World Cup Final by scoring this hat-trick goal?

Can you identify these England goal scorers from the photographs and clues?!

2.

On 11 July 2022, who scored her 58th and final England goal against Norway in an 8-0 victory for the Lionesses at UEFA Women's Euro 2022?

3.

On 31 July 2022, who scored England's extra-time winner against Germany in the UEFA Women's Euro 2022 Final?

4.

Which Bath-born defender scored his first England goal in a 10-0 victory over San Marino on 15 November 2021?

5.

England beat Brazil 4-2 on penalties in the 2023 Women's Finalissima on 6 April 2023. But who scored for the Lionesses during the regulation 90 minutes of that match, which finished in a 1-1 draw?

6.

Who scored his first international goal of 2023 from the penalty spot in a 2-1 victory away to Italy in UEFA Euro 2024 qualifying on 23 March 2023?

7.

Who scored her first England goal in a 4-0 win over South Korea in the Arnold Clark Cup on 16 February 2023?

8.

Who scored England's sixth goal in their 6-1 victory over Belgium in the Arnold Clark Cup on 22 February 2023?

9.

Which Coventry-born forward scored a penalty in England's 4-0 win away to Malta on 16 June 2023 in UEFA Euro 2024 qualifying?

10.

Which Liverpool-born defender also scored in England's 4-0 win away to Malta on 16 June 2023?

BEHIND THE SCENES AT THE HOME OF ENGLAND

The new Wembley Stadium opened in 2007, replacing the original venue which had been in situ between 1923 and 2000. It is the national stadium of England, the home of English football and the largest sports venue in the UK with a capacity of 90,000. It has staged many iconic events over the years including the finals of the UEFA Champions League, UEFA European Championships and UEFA Women's European Championships while it hosts the Emirates FA Cup Final, the Vitality Women's FA Cup Final, Carabao Cup Final and EFL Play-Off Finals on an annual basis.

Let's take a look behind the scenes at this iconic home of English football.

THE ARCH & BOBBY MOORE

Wembley's iconic arch is 133 meters tall and 315 meters wide and is visible from many parts of London and further afield. Many visitors to the Home of Football arrive at Wembley Stadium via Wembley Park London Underground station and walk to the ground along Olympic Way (often referred to as Wembley Way). A statue of England's 1966 World Cup-winning captain Bobby Moore - designed by artist Philip Jackson - overlooks Olympic Way and is a fitting tribute to one of the country's greatest footballing heroes.

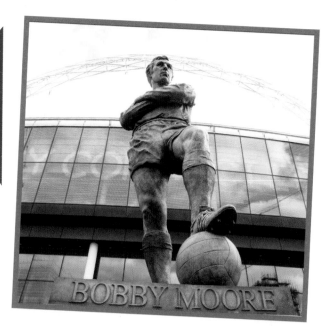

DRESSING ROOMS

Wembley has four dressing rooms, making it suitable for hosting events other than association football matches such as NFL and multi-artist concerts including the Capital FM Summertime Ball. The England national teams always use Dressing Room 2 and their visitors use Dressing Room 1. The squad will arrive 75 minutes in advance of playing a friendly and 90 minutes prior to a FIFA World Cup or UEFA European Championships qualifier.

PLAYERS' TUNNEL

The dressing rooms are situated on the north side of Wembley Stadium, as is the venue's famous Players' Tunnel. Prior to kick-off, players come out of the dressing rooms doors and stand side by side with their opponents in a large area just behind the Players' Tunnel. There will often be mascots for the game and when there are, the players take their hands and walk out onto the pitch together. There has been no shortage of legendary players to have made the walk along the Players' Tunnel over the years including Lionel Messi, Cristiano Ronaldo, Neymar, Gareth Bale, Harry Kane, Raheem Sterling, Wayne Rooney, David Beckham, Leah Williamson and Lucy Bronze.

PITCH

Wembley's pitch has 75,000km of artificial grass fibres stitched in - enough to reach around the world 1.5 times - ensuring an immaculate playing surface all year round. At 105x68m, the pitch is one of the largest in the country. When concerts are held at Wembley, the grass is covered with a special panel system which allows it to continue to breathe and grow and protects it from the thousands of music lovers standing above it!

ROYAL BOX

The original Wembley Stadium was famed for its 39 steps, which both the winning and losing teams in major cup finals would ascend to collect their medals and the trophy from the Royal Box. The new venue also has a Royal Box, which hosts Guests of Honour on match days and which is accessed by climbing 107 steps to meet dignitaries and get their hands on the all-important silverware!

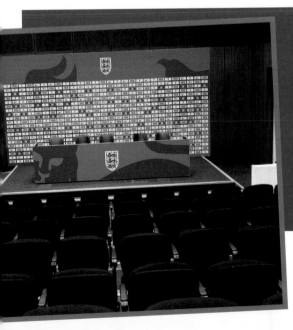

PRESS CONFERENCE ROOM

The Wembley Stadium Press Room is the largest in the United Kingdom, with some 196 seats. After a match, both managers will sit behind the Press Room desk and take questions from the invited national and international media. It was here in July 2022 that England's Lionesses famously gate-crashed Sarina Wiegman's press conference after they had won UEFA Euro 2022, as they danced around the desk - while Lucy Bronze and Mary Earps even climbed on top of it! - and sang Three Lions (Football's Coming Home).

You can go behind the scenes at Wembley Stadium and experience the home of English football on a Wembley Stadium Tour. For more information and to book, visit www.wembleystadium.com/tours

UEFA EURO 2024

The 17th edition of the UEFA European Championships will be held in Germany between 14 June and 14 July 2024. 10 cities will host the action, including Cologne, Stuttgart, Dortmund and Berlin with the final being staged at Olympiastadion Berlin.

TOURNAMENT HISTORY

The first UEFA European Championship Finals took place in 1960, when it was known as the European Nations' Cup, and included only four teams; the host nation France, Czechoslovakia, Yugoslavia and the Soviet Union who were victors.

The idea for a pan-European football tournament had first been mooted 33 years earlier by the French Football Federation's Secretary General Henri Delaunay. He'd passed away by the time the competition was finally launched but the trophy was named in his honour.

The tournament, which takes place every four years, was expanded to include eight teams ahead of the 1980 edition and by Euro 1996, which was hosted in England, 16 nations were taking part. The number of teams involved increased again in 2016, to 24.

THREE LIONS AT THE EUROS

England's first foray into the tournament was in 1968, when they finished third after beating the Soviet Union 2-0 in the play-off game.

In total, the Three Lions have competed at 10 European Championships so far with their best performance coming at the delayed Euro 2020 where they finished as runners-up, having lost to Italy on penalties in the final at Wembley Stadium.

PAST HOSTS/WINNERS

Year	Hosts	Winners
1960	France	Soviet Union
1964	Spain	Spain
1968	Italy	Italy
1972	Belgium	West Germany
1976	Yugoslavia	Czechoslovakia
1980	Italy	West Germany
1984	France	France
1988	West Germany	Netherlands
1992	Sweden	Denmark
1996	England	Germany
2000	Belgium/Netherlands	France
2004	Portugal	Greece
2008	Austria/Switzerland	Spain
2012	Poland/Ukraine	Spain
2016	France	Portugal
2020	11 nations	Italy

To mark the 60th anniversary of competition, 11 cities in 11 UEFA countries provided venues for those finals with the 24 qualified teams competing in six groups of four. The tournament was originally meant to have been played in the summer of 2020 but due to the Covid-19 pandemic it was postponed until June and July 2021.

England reached the semi-finals on home turf at Euro '96 but were defeated by Germany in a penalty shootout. In 2004 and 2012 they progressed to the quarter-finals but lost both games on penalties again.

The Three Lions were drawn in Group C alongside Italy, North Macedonia and Malta for Euro 2024 qualification which began back in March 2023.

ANSWERS

CROSSWORD
Page 32

```
          ¹R
      ²M  I  N  G     ³S
          C           A
          E           K
          ⁴S  ⁵H  A  W
              E
              N
          ⁶M  A  D  D  I  S  O  N
              E
              R
          ⁷P  S
      ⁸W  I  L  S  O  N
  ⁹G       C     ⁰
  R        K  ¹⁰K  A  N  E
  E        F
  A        O
  ¹W  A  L  K  E  R  D
  I        R
  S        D
  ¹R  A  S  H  F  O  R  D
```

WORDSEARCH
Page 33

```
T G R E E N W O O D R E O A
A L E R S W G Y T O W A T E
S O A K E L L Y S W E R E N
A S W R T H G I R B N M H G
S R U S S O N S W A L S H L
T B E Y H O C O O M B S C A
O E O G H L T O E G W M S N
T E Y S L T W O S N O O L D
S L A N W Y A W T O O A N O
S D S R O C A N A O A T E S
S G N N P E G G N T O O N E
L O H W S S A A W E R Y D O
W A A B T G G P A O L T T T
O D S D E W A S Y S R D I S
```

60

QUIZ

Page 40-41

1. 1966	16. Group D
2. UEFA Europa Conference League	17. 17
3. 107	18. Real Madrid
4. 24	19. Ian Foster
5. Portugal	20. Spain
6. 1996	21. Nottingham
7. Italy	22. Ukraine
8. Tottenham Hotspur	23. Giles Moore
9. Millie Bright	24. Bobby Moore
10. Scotland	25. Bristol City
11. Women's Finalissima	26. Bukayo Saka
12. Marcus Rashford	27. Beth Mead
13. Birmingham	28. 54
14. Australia	29. Netherlands
15. Haiti	30. 2022

GUESS THE GOALSCORER

Page 52

1. Geoff Hurst	6. Harry Kane
2. Ellen White	7. Lauren James
3. Chloe Kelly	8. Leah Williamson
4. Tyrone Mings	9. Callum Wilson
5. Ella Toone	10. Trent Alexander-Arnold

SPOT THE PLAYERS

Can you spot the four lions and four lionesses hiding in the crowd at Wembley?